中文
入门

CHINESE FOR BEGINNERS

中文入门

BY LIU XIAOYU
刘晓雨 编著

北京大学出版社
PEKING UNIVERSITY PRESS

图书在版编目（CIP）数据

中文入门=Chinese for Beginners / 刘晓雨编著.— 北京：北京大学出版社
2016.9

ISBN 978-7-301-27225-1

Ⅰ.①中… Ⅱ.①刘… Ⅲ.①汉语—口语—对外汉语教学—教材 Ⅳ.①H195.4

中国版本图书馆CIP数据核字(2016)第136979号

书　　名 中文入门
ZHONGWEN RUMEN

著作责任者 刘晓雨 编著

责任编辑 孙娴

标准书号 ISBN 978-7-301-27225-1

出版发行 北京大学出版社

地　　址 北京市海淀区成府路205号　100871

网　　址 http://www.pup.cn　　新浪微博：@北京大学出版社

电子信箱 zpup@pup.cn

电　　话 邮购部 62752015　发行部 62750672　编辑部 62753027

印 刷 者 北京大学印刷厂

经 销 者 新华书店

787毫米×960毫米　32开本　3.375印张　54千字

2016年9月第1版　2016年9月第1次印刷

定　　价 45.00元

PREFACE

Chinese for Beginners is the first Chinese language MOOC for global learners on Coursera - one of the most famous platforms of MOOC. It was prepared since May 2014 and the target of the course is to help beginners to understand and speak some basic sentences and vocabularies. Since it was published online on September 2014, there are more than 650,000 visitors and more than 300,000 active learners from more than 200 countries and regions by August 2016.

The course is designed for global beginners and the teaching language is English. All those who have a basic level of English can join the course. Chinese character is a big problem for almost all learners according to our teaching experiences. That's why the content of the course is totally given in *Pinyin.*

Chinese for Beginners is an on-demand course. The demands of the learners are very different because of their countries, ages, genders, mother languages, cultural and educational backgrounds, occupations, purposes, etc. But there are some common topics in people's social life. 7 selected topics and situations in this course come from real life scenarios, including personal information, food and drink, time, shopping, living environment, health, and hobby. The learner can finish the course within 7-8 weeks, learning 4 lessons of 1 unit per week.

The teaching video of each lesson is in no more than 5 minutes.

The sentences are in very basic S+V+O pattern as far as possible, and the positive and negative answers are given accordingly. The learners will find Chinese language structure is not that different and difficult at the elementary level in spite of some special characteristics. They can learn the basic sentences and then express with some common vocabulary substitutions. Besides the daily dialogues, there are some brief introductions of Chinese initials, finals, tones for learners who need to know the phonetic situation when they learn Chinese. Some exercises including listening, reading and tongue twisters are given to help the learners to understand that some mistakes could bring misunderstanding such as "Wǒ xiǎng wèn nǐ"(I want to ask you) and "Wǒ xiǎng wěn nǐ"(I want to kiss you).

Many active learners around the world contribute much to the course enthusiastically in their own way, such as making word and expression lists, giving constructive advices to improve the course. A lot of learners even ask for paper materials, because they would like to reflect on the system of the knowledge. They are used to taking notes while learning, and flipping frequently to check their learning outcomes.

They are eager to have a further reading and curious about the scripts of those common words in the course. Therefore, the coordinated textbook of *Chinese for Beginners* is now published.

The textbook is completely faithful to the MOOC *Chinese for Beginners*. Besides, it summarizes over 180 essential words on numbers (time, prices), colors, food, seasons, health, sports and internet scattered in different units, and provides the vocabulary list with Chinese character, *Pinyin*, English and Spanish to help learners to review and prepare for the advanced course. Those who are interested in Chinese characters can observe and try to understand the characteristic of Chinese language and culture. It also provides some explanations of the key points and related Chinese social situation.

What's more, the textbook is designed in a small size so that the online self-study course can be used anytime anywhere offline. Leaners can not only study the Chinese offline, but also scan the QR code offered by the book to watch the teaching videos online.

For some ultra-short-time Chinese training program, such as study tours, teachers may be worried about suitable teaching materials. This simple and concise textbook is a good choice. With a complete set of teaching videos, the teaching approaches could be more flexible. For instance, teachers may organize a flipped classroom by encouraging the students to learn the course themselves first outside the class, then answering their questions and adding more interactive oral exercises. We believe that will be an efficient way.

We have a lot of wonderful experiences in the process of making the MOOC *Chinese for Beginners*. There is an Indian learner, for example, who learned the course, and came to China, to Beijing, to Peking University, even to School of Chinese as a Second Language! The people who have no chance to meet at all now have some person-to-person connection because of MOOC. What a magic! We hope through this coordinated textbook of MOOC, we can build a connection with you as well. Let's enjoy the Chinese-learning experiences together!

Liu Xiaoyu
Zhang Guang Yuan
August 24, 2016

序

“Chinese for Beginners”入门级课程于2014年5月筹划，2014年9月选择在世界三大MOOC(慕课)平台之一的Coursera平台上线，因为这里注册学习者最多、开的课程也最多。“Chinese for Beginners”是该平台上第一门中文语言课，也是国内第一门面向全球以培养交际能力为目的的汉语语言慕课。这门课程专门针对零起点汉语学习者设计，以听说为主，受到了广泛的关注与认同。截至2016年8月，已经有200多个国家和地区的65万人访问，活跃的学习者超过30万。

既然是面向全球开设的汉语入门级网络课程，我们选择以英语为授课语言，既利用了英语在全球的语言优势，也没有影响其他母语地区的学习者参与课程，学习者只要具备基本的英语水平就可以听课。根据二十多年零起点口语教学的经验，我们理解汉字对绝大多数学习者的困难程度，而大胆采用全拼音教学，完全不涉及汉字。

不同国家或地区、不同年龄和性别、不同语言和文化背景、不同教育程度和职业，不同的学习目的，学习者的需求千差万别。尽管如此，社会生活中总有一些普适性的话题。我们从真实生活场景中精选了7个话题作为教学单元，包括个人信息、饮食、时间、购物、居住环境、健康、爱好等。为了让学习者相对容易地完成课程，找到自己最感兴趣的内容或最需要解决的问题，整个课程我们设计的教学周期仅仅7周，每周1个单元，每单元4课，每课以简单日常会话为主，教学视频不超过5分钟，知识点都进行了碎片化处理。

我们希望入门级的学习者能够看到，汉语最基本的表达方式并不难，所以会话内容尽可能地只包含基本的主—谓—宾成分，以问答方式展现疑问、肯定回答和否定回答，再辅以几个常用的替换词语，方便学习和使用。当然，学习汉语，总要对汉语特别是语音概况有个大概的了解，所以在第1周的单元里，除了日常会话以外，还介绍了汉语的声母、韵母、声调等基础语音知识，练习形式包括听辨语音、跟读词语和绕口令等，让学习者意识到相似的声调、声母、韵母的不同，发不准会产生误会甚至闹笑话，比如“我想问你”和“我想吻你”。

五湖四海的学习者对汉语的学习热情令我们感动，他们自发地制作常用词表，总结基本语法点，提出完善课程的合理建议。很多学习者向我们索要纸质教材，因为他们想看到课程内部的系统性，因为他们习惯了一边学习一边做笔记，因为他们希望随时翻看复习检测自己的学习效果，因为他们渴求深度阅读，因为他们想了解这些常用词的汉字是什么样的……于是，课程的同步配套教材《中文入门》诞生了。

这本教材完全忠实于我们的课程，同时，还补充了一些阅读材料，学习者可以进一步了解什么是普通话、汉语拼音方案、拼音拼写规则、语音变调等等。汉语的“一”“不”和第三声音节在说话时变来变去，初学者往往不得要领，很难分辨理解，教材系统地帮助他们梳理了这方面的相关知识。课程里涉及数字（时间、价格）、颜色、饮食、季节、病症、运动、上网等方面的常用词语180多个，分散在不同的地方，我们在教材里做了汇总，并为每个词语提供了汉字、拼音、英文和西班牙文注释，制作成常用词表。这样既方便学习者检索复习，为进阶课程做好准备，又可以让有兴趣的学习者观察一下汉字，体会汉语言和文字的特点。另外，学习的重难点、相关文化背景也通过教材得到了展示。

特别值得一提的是，课程的适用范围也借助教材得到了延伸。原本是网络自学课程，如今线上线下的通道被打开了。教材采用小开本设计，轻便而易携带，学习者在线下可以随时随地翻阅学习。教材里每课开始的地方都有一个二维码，学习者遇到不明白的地方，打开手机扫一扫，线上对应的课程视频可以即时播放。

一些超短期的汉语培训项目，比如游学，教师们常常苦于没有适用的教学材料。我们这本教材的内容短小精悍，可以说是一个不错的选择。由于有完整配套的课程视频，教学形式也可以更为灵活多样。鼓励学生课下自学，再组织翻转课堂，集中答疑解惑，增加些口头表达的互动练习，相信会取得很好的教学效果。

筹划、制作、维护“Chinese for Beginners”课程的过程中，我们收获了很多奇妙的体验：有一位印度的学习者，看了我们的慕课，很想感受一下中国，就来到了北京，来到了北京大学，还找到了对外汉语教育学院！本来一生中绝不可能有交集的人，现在因慕课而有了某种联系。希望这本与课程同步配套的教材《中文入门》也能建立起我们和你之间的联系，让我们一起分享汉语学习的乐趣！

刘晓雨

2016年8月24日于中关园

CONTENTS

Unit 1

Who are you?

When we first meet someone, we need to learn about each other. In this unit, we are going to learn some ways to introduce yourself, including name, nationality, identity, and discussing your family. We are also going to study Chinese Mandarin phonetics.

中文入门

Chinese For Beginners

Who are you?

PAGE

1-1

What is your name?

Dialogues

01

A: Nǐ hǎo!

(Hello.)

B: Nǐ hǎo!

(Hello.)

02

A: Nǐ jiào shénme míngzi?

(What's your name?)

B: Wǒ jiào ……

(My name is …)

03

Xièxie!

(Thank you.)

Zàijiàn!

(See you.)

Tones

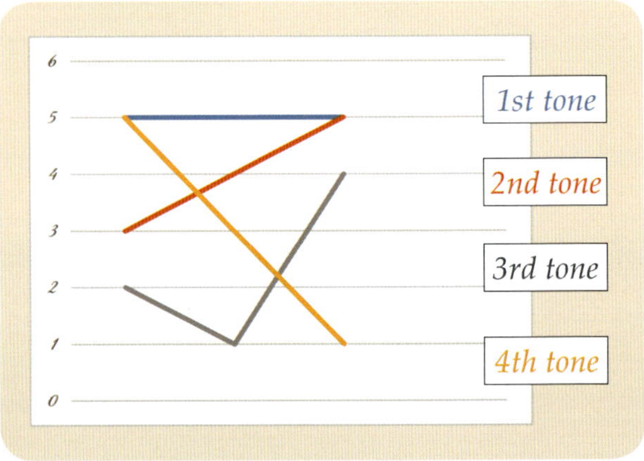

Simple finals

ā	á	ǎ	à
ō	ó	ǒ	ò
ē	é	ě	è
ī	í	ǐ	ì

ū	ú	ǔ	ù
ǖ	ǘ	ǚ	ǜ

Notes

Tones can distinguish meaning in Chinese. If tones are pronounced wrongly, some jokes will be made. If you want to say "I want to ask you", the correct way is "Wǒ xiǎng wèn nǐ" and not "Wǒ xiǎng wěn nǐ *(I want to kiss you)*"!

Exercise

Can you try to read the following tongue twister correctly?

Māma qímǎ. Mǎ màn. Māma mà mǎ.

(Mum is riding a horse. The horse goes slowly. Mum scolds the horse.)

Recommending reading

Mandarin Chinese

The common language of the Han nationality is Mandarin Chinese. Mandarin is also the official language of the People's Republic of China. Beijing phonetic is regarded as the standard pronunciation and the basic dialect is the dialect of the northern part of the country. The standard modern Chinese written works become grammar examples.

Generally speaking, a single Chinese character is equal to a syllable. The structure of a Chinese syllable is quite simple, usually being composed of an initial and a final with a tone. The initial is the first part of a syllable. Following the initial is the final, which can be classified into three types; the simple final, compound final and final with a nasal ending. Tone marks are placed on the major vowels of the final.

1-8

Where are you from?

Dialogue

01

A: Nǐ shì nǎ guó rén?

(Where's are you from?)

B: Wǒ shì Yīngguórén.

(I'm from UK.)

Pronouns

	Déguó	Germany
	Fǎguó	France
	Měiguó	USA
	Rìběn	Japan
	Xībānyá	Spain
	Yìndù	India
	Zhōngguó	China

Initials

b	p	m	f
d	t	n	l
g	k	h	
j	q	x	
zh	ch	sh	r
z	c	s	

Exercise

Please pronounce the following words and the tongue twister correctly:

① qìchē *(car)* zìjǐ *(self)*

- rìjì *(diary)* sījī *(driver)*
- jìzhě *(journalist)* chūzūchē *(taxi)*
- zìxíngchē *(bike)* zìzhùcān *(buffet)*

② Sì shì sì, shí shì shí. Shísì shì shísì, sìshí shì sìshí.

(4 is 4, 10 is 10, 14 is 14, 40 is 40.)

Recommending reading

Pinyin

The *Pinyin* is a system for representing standard Mandarin in the Latin alphabet. It contains 26 letters, 21 initials, 39 finals, 4 tones and several special spelling rules.

In 1610, a French missionary first used the Latin alphabet to record the pronunciation of Chinese characters. Then in 1958, Chinese government published the "Scheme for the Chinese Phonetic Alphabet" officially. Later in 1977, the United Nation adopted *Pinyin* as the international spelling standards of Chinese geographical names and the scheme became ISO 7098 (Roman alphabet spellings for Chinese) in 1982.

The *Pinyin* has become the educational-based content in Chinese mainland and a essential part in Chinese-speaking communities overseas.

The laws of Chinese *Pinyin* are relatively simple, which plays an important in popularizing Chinese characters and primary education. With the popularization of computer technology, *Pinyin* has become a very popular Chinese input method besides character stroke input.

Because *Pinyin* is only for recording the pronunciation, it can never be the substitute of Chinese character. The article that completely written by *Pinyin* is difficult to understand. Therefore, *Pinyin* is not a formal way of writing and it is just a reading aid.

Are you a student?

Dialogues

01

A: Nǐ shì xuésheng ma?

(Are you a student?)

B: Duì, wǒ shì xuésheng.

(Right, I'm a student.)

Bù, wǒ bú shì xuésheng.

(No. I'm not a student.)

Wǒ shì lǎoshī.

(I'm a teacher.)

02

A: Nǐ xuéxí shénme?

(What do you study?)

B: Wǒ xuéxí Hànyǔ.

(I study Chinese.)

Compound finals

ai	ei	ao	ou	
ia	ie	ua	uo	üe
iao	iou	uai	uei	

Notes

1. "ma" can be used at the end of any statement to make a question such as:

Wǒ shì Zhōngguórén. + ma

→

Nǐ shì Zhōngguórén ma?

2. Have you notice the tone changes of "bù(no/not)"? Please check the rules in "Recommending reading" of Lesson 1-4.

3. When we make a question, we don't need to change the order of the expression as in English.

① Nǐ jiào shénme míngzi?

Wǒ jiào Liú Xiǎoyǔ.

② Nǐ shì nǎ guó rén?

Wǒ shì Fǎguórén.

③ Nǐ xuéxí shénme?

Wǒ xuéxí Hànyǔ.

Exercise 1

Can you try to read the following tongue twister correctly?

Jiāojiao zǎo qǐ jiào jiùjiu. Kuài bēi yóulǒu mǎi lǒu yóu.

(Jiaojiao gets up early and calls her uncle to get a basket carried on the back to buy some oil.)

Recommending reading

Rules of spelling

1. The finals of zhi, chi, shi, ri, zi, ci, si are all written as i.

zhi chi shi ri zi ci si

2. Finals beginning with i without initials are written as:

yi ya ye yao you yan yin yang ying yong

3. Finals beginning with u without initials are written as:

wu wa wo wai wei wan wen wang weng

4. ü and üe are combined with l and n, the two dots on the ü are remained.

lü nü lüe nü

When ü and finals beginning with ü are combined with j, q, x, ü is all written as u.

ju quan xue

5. When the finals beginning with ü without initials, the two dots on the ü are omitted, these are written as:

yu yue yuan yun

6. When iou, uei, uen are preceded by initials, they are written as iu, ui, un.

niu liu gui hun

7. Tone marks are marked on the vowels ɑ, o, e, i, u, ü according to the order. When the tone mark is on an i, the dot on the i can be omitted.

kāi zhǎo tiào guā tiē zǒu jīn bēi cuò juān quē

8. For the finals iu and ui, the tone marks should be placed on the latter u or i.

diū huì

1-4

Who is he/she?

Dialogues

01

Zhè shì wǒ *(This is my...)*	bàba *(father)*	.
	māma *(mother)*	

02

A: Tā shì shéi?
(Who is he/she?)

B: Tā shì wǒ *(He/She is my...)*	jiějie *(elder sister)*	.
	mèimei *(younger sister)*	
	dìdi *(younger brother)*	
	gēge *(elder brother)*	

Finals with nasal endings

an	ian	uan	üan
ang	iang	uang	
en	in	uen	ün
eng	ing	ueng	
ong	iong		

Exercise

Try to read the following words and tongue twister correctly.

① shāngdiàn *(shop)* yínháng *(bank)*

- míngtiān *(tomorrow)* dēnglong *(lantern)*
- rénshēng *(life)* wǎnfàn *(supper)*
- chènshān *(shirt)* gōngyuán *(park)*

② Hóng fènghuáng, fěn fènghuáng.

Hóngfěn fènghuáng, fěnhóng fènghuáng.

Huáng fènghuáng.

(Red phoenix, pink phoenix.

Red and pink phoenix, pink and red phoenix.

yellow phoenix.)

Recommending reading

Sound Change

1. Tone changes

Third tone sandhi

When two 3rd tones are next to each other, the first one changes into the 2nd tone.

nǐ hǎo – ní hǎo

It happens when we speak and hear but we won't change the tone mark when we write.

Tone change of "yī (one)"

When it is read independently or is at the end

of a word, "yī (one)" is pronounced as yī;

When it precedes a 1st, 2nd or a 3rd tone, it is pronounced as yì.

yì+tiān – one+day
yì+nián – one+year
yì+běn – one+*measure word for book*

When it precedes a 4th tone, it is pronounced as yí.

yí bàn – a half

Tone changes of "bù (no/not)"

The tone of "bù (no/not)" does not change when it stands by itself or precedes a 1st, 2nd or a 3rd tone, pronounced as bù.

bù tīng – not listen
bù lái – not come
bù xiǎng – not think

It is pronounced as bú when it precedes a 4th tone.

bú yào – not want

2. The neutral tone

The neutral tone is not the fifth tone. It's just a soft and short sound when a syllabus lost its original tone. The neutral tone has not a certain tone pitch. There is not any tone mark above the neutral syllabus because the tone pitch will be chosen up to the tone of the syllabus before it. The neutral tone has a relationship with grammar such as "le", "de". Sometimes it may identify the meaning of the word, such as "dōngxī" (*n. east and west*) and "dōngxi" (*n. things*), "mǎimài" (*v. buy and sell*) and "mǎimai"(*n. business*). The second syllabus of some disyllabic words is also read in the neutral tone, such as "xuésheng".

shénme (what)
bàba (father)
míngzi (name)
wǒ de (my)

3. The retroflex final

"-r" is not only a kind of phonetic phenomena, sometimes it can change the meaning or the grammatic function of the word, such as:

huà (*v.* to draw)
huàr (*n.* picture)
yǎn (*n.* eye)
yǎnr (*n.* small hole)

nouns with "-r" generally indicates the meaning of "small, cute ", such as:

xiǎoháir (little kid)
huār (lovely flower)

Can you pronounce correctly?

character

1-2

zhì ✗

zì ✓

China

1-2

Chōngguó ✗

1-4

Zhēngguó ✗

Zhōngguó ✓

Chinese language

1-4

Hàngyǔ ✗

Hànyǔ ✓

India

Yìngdù ✗

1-4

✓ Yìndù

Japanese

Lìběnlén ✗

1-2

Rìběngréng ✗

1-4

✓ Rìběnrén

name

mínzi ✗

1-4

✓ míngzi

Spain

1-4

Xībāngyá ✗

✓ Xībānyá

student

1-4

xuéshen ✗

1-4

xuéshong ✗

✓ xuésheng

to be

1-4

xì ✗

1-4

sì ✗

✓ shì

to call

zhào ✗

1-2

ziào ✗

✓ jiào

1-2

to thank

shè ✗

✓ xiè

1-2

to visit

zhàn ✗

✓ jiàn

1-2

UK
Yīnguó ✗
1-4
✓ Yīngguó

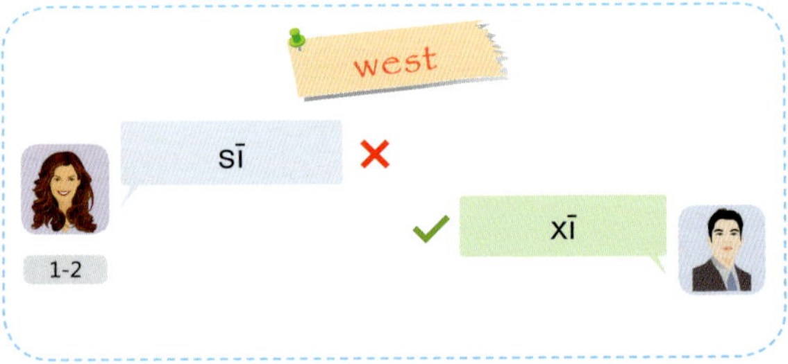
west
sī ✗
1-2
✓ xī

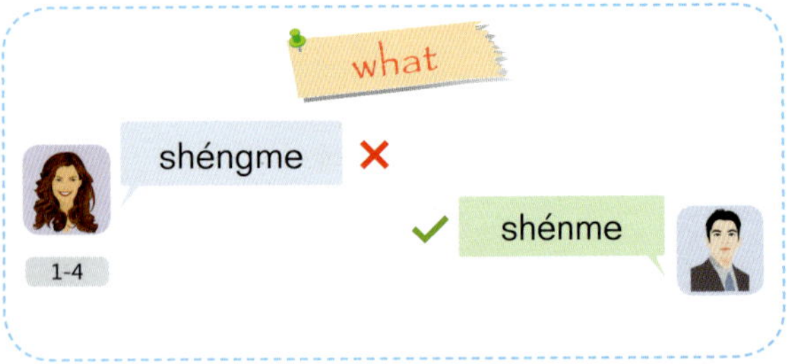
what
shéngme ✗
1-4
✓ shénme

Unit 2

When do you go to school?

How do you plan your daily life? In this unit, we are going to learn how to describe our daily schedule, including numbers, time, periods, and some corresponding actions.

中文入门
Chinese For Beginners

When do you go to school?

PAGE

Can you count?

Numbers

1	2	3	4	5
yī	èr	sān	sì	wǔ

6	7	8	9	10
liù	qī	bā	jiǔ	shí

11 (10 + 1)

shíyī (shí + yī)
(jiā)

12 (10 + 2)

shí'èr (shí + èr)
(jiā)

13

(+)
(jiā)

14

(+)
(jiā)

20 (2 × 10)

èrshí (èr × shí)
(chéng)

21 (2 × 10 + 1)

èrshíyī (èr × shí + yī)

(chéng) (jiā)

22

(× +)

(chéng) (jiā)

23

(× +)

(chéng) (jiā)

30 40

sānshí sìshí

50 60

70 80 90

2-2

What time is it now?

Time(o'clock)

1:00	yì diǎn
2:00	liǎng diǎn
3:00	sān diǎn
4:00	
5:00	
6:00	
7:00	
8:00	

Notes

If we want to tell there are 2 something, we need to say "liǎng" before the measure word instead of "èr" such as:

liǎng diǎn *(two o'clock)*
liǎng tiān *(two days)*
liǎng kuài *(two dollars)*

Dialogue

01

A: Qǐngwèn, xiànzài jǐ diǎn?

(Excuse me, what time is it now?)

B: Xiànzài shí'èr diǎn.

(It's 12 o'clock now.)

2-3

Morning or afternoon?

Time(period)

zǎoshang	early morning
shàngwǔ	morning
zhōngwǔ	noon
xiàwǔ	afternoon
wǎnshang	evening

6:00 — 6:00 a.m.

zǎoshang liù diǎn

10:00 — 10:00 a.m.

shàngwǔ shí diǎn

12:00

zhōngwǔ shí'èr diǎn

1:00 p.m.

xiàwǔ yì diǎn

2:00 p.m.

xiàwǔ liǎng diǎn

8:00 p.m.

wǎnshang bā diǎn

Notes

In China, it is conventional to follow the rule of general to specific when expressing date, address and name. For example, we express date by the order of

"year – month – day – period (morning or afternoon) – time (o'clock)" .

Address is expressed as

"country – province – city – district – road – building – room" .

And my name is

Liú *(family name)* Xiǎoyǔ *(personal name).*

Do you have a busy life?

Expressions

1. Wǒ zǎoshang liù diǎn qǐchuáng.

   (I get up at six in the morning.)

2. Wǒ zǎoshang qī diǎn chī zǎofàn.

   (I have the breakfast at seven in the morning.)

3. Wǒ shàngwǔ jiǔ diǎn gōngzuò.

   (I go to work at nine in the morning.)

4. Wǒ zhōngwǔ shí'èr diǎn chī wǔfàn.

   (I have the lunch at twelve o'clock.)

5. Wǒ xiàwǔ liù diǎn huíjiā.

   (I go home at six in the afternoon.)

6. Wǒ wǎnshang bā diǎn chī wǎnfàn.

   (I have the dinner at eight in the evening.)

7. Wǒ wǎnshang shíyī diǎn shuìjiào.

   (I go to sleep at eleven in the evening.)

Notes

When we want to say: "somebody is doing something in some certain time", we express it by the order of "someone – time – action", which is different to English.

Unit 3

What do you like to eat?

Food is our most important need. In this unit, we are going to talk about Chinese main courses, fruits, vegetables and meat, as well as drinks. Have you seen or tried any of these Chinese dishes? Maybe you have already learned to say them in Chinese!

中文入门

Chinese For Beginners

What do you like to eat?

PAGE

Do you like dumpling?

Dialogues

01

A: Nǐ chī shénme?

(What do you want to eat?)

B: Wǒ chī *(I eat)*

jiǎozi	*(dumpling)*
chǎomiàn	*(fried noodle)*
chǎofàn	*(fried rice)*
miàntiáo	*(noodle)*

.

02

A: Nǐ chī jiǎozi ma?

(Do you eat dumpling?)

B: Wǒ bù chī jiǎozi.

(No, I don't.)

Wǒ chī bāozi.

(I eat filled, steamed bun.)

Notes

There are hundreds of different kind of noodle in China. "miàntiáo" is the general name and sometimes the name for the noodle with plain soup.

I like apple.

Dialogues

01

A: Nǐ xǐhuan shénme shuǐguǒ?

(What fruit do you like?)

B: Wǒ xǐhuan *(I like)*	píngguǒ *(apple)* / xiāngjiāo *(banana)* / chéngzi *(orange)*	.

02

A: Nǐ xǐhuan píngguǒ ma?

(Do you like apple ?)

B: Wǒ bù xǐhuan píngguǒ.

(No, I don't.)

Wǒ xǐhuan xiāngjiāo.

(I like banana.)

Notes

About the pronunciation of "shuǐguǒ", please check the rules of "Third tone sandhi" in "Recommending reading" of Lesson 1-4.

I like chicken.

Dialogues

01

A: Nǐ yào shénme?

(What do you want?)

B: Wǒ yào *(I want)*

niúròu	*(beef)*	
jīròu	*(chicken)*	
zhūròu	*(pork)*	.
yú	*(fish)*	
shūcài	*(vegetables)*	

  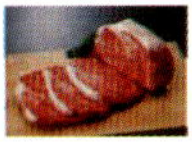  

02

A: Nǐ yào niúròu ma?

(Do you want beef?)

B: Wǒ bú yào niúròu.

(No, I don't.)

Wǒ yào shūcài.

(I want vegetables.)

3-4

Do you want a cup of tea?

Dialogues

01

A: Nǐ hē shénme?

(What do you drink?)

B: Wǒ hē shuǐ *(water)* / kělè *(coke)* / kāfēi *(coffee)* / chá *(tea)* / píjiǔ *(beer)* .

02

A: Nǐ hē shuǐ ma?

(Do you drink water?)

B: wǒ bù hē shuǐ.

(No, I don't.)

Wǒ hē kělè.

(I drink coke.)

Unit 4

I like shopping!

Shopping! Shopping! Some people love to go shopping, while others feel it is a headache. Still, shopping is an essential part of our life. In this unit, we are going to learn how to express our color and size preference, how to ask about price, and how to bargain. Do you know what the most popular color is in your country? How about in China?

中文入门
Chinese For Beginners

I like shopping!

PAGE

What is your favorite color?

Colors

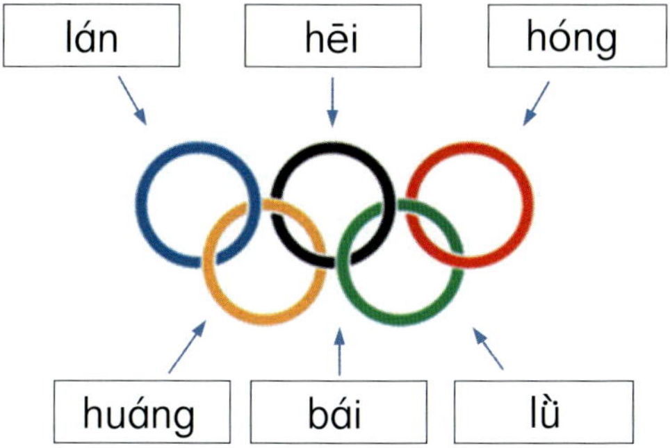

Dialogue

01

A: Nǐ xǐhuan shénme yánsè?

(What color do you like?)

B: Wǒ xǐhuan hóng de.

(I like red.)

Notes

Red is a very popular color in China. It usually appears on wedding, festival celebration, opening of a new business, etc. .

This is too big.

Dialogues

01

A: Zhè ge zěnmeyàng?

(What do you think of this?)

B: Wǒ bù xǐhuan zhè ge.

(I don't like this one.)

Wǒ xǐhuan nà ge.

(I like that one.)

02

A: Zhè jiàn zěnmeyàng?

(What do you think of this?)

B: Zhè jiàn tài dà le.

(This is too large.)

Wǒ yào nà jiàn xiao de.

(I want that small one.)

Notes

1. "tài … le" means "very, extremely". For example:

① Tài hǎo le! (*Great!*)

② Tài hēi le. (*It's too black.*)

③ Tài xiǎo le. (*It's too small.*)

2. The "de" phrases are composed of "…+ de". The word before "de" can be a noun, an pronoun, a verb, an adjective and so on.The "de" phrase acts as one noun.

① Zhèxiē xuésheng shì Měiguó de.
(*These students are American.*)

② Zhè běn shū shì wǒ de.
(*This is my book.*)

③ Tā mǎi de guì. Wǒ mǎi de piányi.
(*The one he bought is expensive. The one I bought is cheap.*)

④ Wǒ yào xiǎo de.
(*I want the small one.*)

How much is this?

Price

kuài *(unit of the currency—RMB in China)*

1.00	yí kuài
2.00	liǎng kuài
5.00	
10.00	

¥ 20.00

¥ 50.00

¥ 100.00 yìbǎi *(hundred)* kuài

Notes

1. The portrait on the paper money, which is called "rénmínbì" *(RMB)*, is Máo Zédōng", the first leader of the People' s Republic of China founded in 1949.

2. Our saying will sound more naturally if we change the tone of "ī" . Please check the rules in "Recommending reading" of Lesson 1-4.

3. We don' t have to give the "be" verb when we tell the time and price. For example:

Xiànzài (shì) shí diǎn. *(It's ten o'clock now.)*

Zhè ge (shì) èrshí kuài. *(This is twenty dollars.)*

There is no "be" verb when we describe something such as:

Nà ge (*shì) tài xiǎo le. *(That one is too small.)*

4. "duōshao" means "how many/how much". We have learned another "how many (jǐ)" — in Lesson 2-2 when we talk about "What time is it now?" Generally speaking, "duōshao" is used to ask any quantity. "jǐ" is used to ask the number which is less than ten.

We usually use the numbers from one to twelve to tell the time. That's why we ask "jǐ diǎn" instead of "duōshao diǎn". For the price, you can ask "duōshao qián" when you have no idea at all. Or you can also ask "jǐ kuài qián" when you know it's quite cheap.

Dialogue

01

A: Qǐngwèn, zhè ge duōshao qián?

(Excuse me, how much is this?)

B: Zhè ge liǎng kuài.

(This is 2 dollars.)

It's too expensive!

Dialogue

01

A: Qǐngwèn, píngguǒ duōshao qián?

(Excuse me, how much are the apples?)

B: Píngguǒ wǔ kuài.

(The apples are five dollars.)

A: Tài guì le!

(It's too expensive!)

Piányi yìdiǎnr, hǎo ma?

(A little cheaper, OK?)

Notes

"yìdiǎnr" (a little) can be used after adjectives to indicate "a little more... than..." . For example:

Zhè ge hǎo yìdiǎnr. *(This one is a little better.)*

Nà ge guì yìdiǎnr. *(That one is a little expensive.)*

Unit 5

Do you live in a big city?

Do you live in a big city or a small town? How do you get to work or school every day? In this unit, we are going to learn how to give directions and how to speak about transportation. This unit is valuable in case you need to talk about directions with a Chinese friend or you need to go somewhere when you are in China.

中文入门

Chinese For Beginners

➤ Do you live in a big city?

PAGE

I go to work by car.

Dialogues

01

A: Měi tiān nǐ zěnme qù xuéxiào?

(How do you go to school every day?)

B: Wǒ *(I)*

- zǒulù *(by walking)*
- qí zìxíngchē *(by bike)*
- zuò dìtiě *(take underground)*

.

02

A: Měi tiān nǐ kāi chē qù gōngzuò ma?

(Do you go to work by car every day?)

B: Wǒ bù kāi chē.

(No, I don't go by car.)

Wǒ zuò gōnggòng qìchē.

(I take the bus.)

5-2 Is there a supermarket near here?

Dialogue

01

A: Qǐngwèn，fùjìn yǒu

(Excuse me. Is there ...near here?)

dìtiězhàn	*(underground station)*	ma?
chāoshì	*(supermarket)*	
shāngdiàn	*(mall)*	
yínháng	*(bank)*	

B: Yǒu，zài nàr.

(Yes, It's over there.)

B: Duìbuqǐ, wǒ bù zhīdào.

(Sorry, I have no idea.)

A: Méi guānxi.

(That's all right.)

It is on the left.

Directions

shàngbian *(up)*

zuǒbian *(left)*

yòubian *(right)*

xiàbian *(down)*

Dialogues

01

A: Shuǐ zài nǎr?

(Where is the water?)

B:

Shuǐ *(water)*	zài	shàngbian *(upward)*	.
Yú *(fish)*		xiàbian *(downward)*	
Kělè *(coke)*		zuǒbian *(left)*	
Shūcài *(vegetable)*		yòubian *(right)*	

02

Tā zài qiánbian.

(It's forward.)

Tā zài hòubian.

(It's backward.)

How can I get to the restroom?

Dialogues

01

A: Qǐngwèn, xǐshǒujiān zài nǎr?

(Excuse me, where is the restroom?)

B: Xǐshǒujiān zài zuǒbian.

(The restroom is on the left.)

A: Xièxie nǐ.

(Thank you.)

B: Bú kèqi.

(You're welcome.)

02

A: Qǐngwèn，fùjìn yǒu chāoshì ma?

(Excuse me, Is there a supermarket near here?)

B: Yǒu，wǎng qián zǒu，wǎng yòu guǎi.

(Yes. Go ahead. Then turn right.)

A: Xièxie nǐ.

(Thank you.)

B: Bú kèqi.

(You're welcome.)

Unit 6

How about the weather?

Weather can influence our daily life and personal health. In this unit, we are going to talk about temperature, seasons, and personal health. China is a very big country and the weather can be quite different across regions and seasons; we will learn to talk about all sorts of weather.

中文入门

Chinese For Beginners

How about the weather?

6-1

What is the temperature today?

Dialogues

01

A: Jīntiān tiānqì zěnmeyàng?

(How about the weather today?)

B: Jīntiān xiàyǔ.

(It's going to rain today.)

Tiānqì bù hǎo.

(The weather is not good.)

02

A: Míngtiān tiānqì hǎo bu hǎo?

(Is tomorrow's weather good or not?)

B: Míngtiān xiàxuě.

(It's going to snow tomorrow.)

Tiānqì hěn lěng.

(It's very cold.)

03

A: Jīntiān duōshao dù?

(What is the temperature today?)

B: Sānshíwǔ dù.

(35℃.)

Tiānqì hěn rè.

(It's very hot.)

Is it cold in January?

Months

yī yuè (Jan.)	èr yuè (Feb.)	sān yuè (Mar.)
sì yuè (Apr.)	wǔ yuè (May)	liù yuè (Jun.)
qī yuè (Jul.)	bā yuè (Aug.)	jiǔ yuè (Sep.)
shí yuè (Oct.)	shíyī yuè (Nov.)	shí 'èr yuè (Dec.)

Dialogues

01

A: Yī yuè tiānqì zěnmeyàng?

(How about the weather in January?)

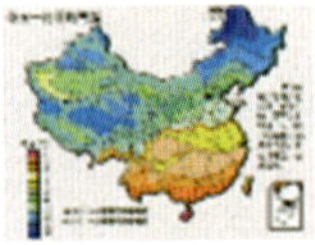

B: Yī yuè tiānqì hěn lěng.

(It's very cold in January.)

02

A: Qī yuè tiānqì hǎo bu hǎo?

(Is the weather fine in July or not?)

B: Qī yuè tiānqì hěn rè.

(It's very hot in July.)

6-3

I like spring.

Dialogues

01

A: Nǐ xǐhuan shénme jìjié?

(What season do you like?)

B: Wǒ xǐhuan

- chūntiān *(spring)*
- xiàtiān *(summer)*
- qiūtiān *(autumn)*
- dōngtiān *(winter)*

.

02

A: Nǐ xǐhuan chūntiān ma?

(Do you like spring?)

B: Xǐhuan.

(Yes, I like it.)

A: Wèi shénme?

(Why?)

B: Yīnwèi chūntiān bù lěng bú rè. Tiānqì hěn hǎo.

(Because it's not cold and not hot. The weather is so good.)

6-4

I catch a cold.

Dialogues

01

A: Nǐ zěnme le?

(What's wrong with you?)

B: Wǒ gǎnmào le.

(I catch a cold.)

Zuótiān tiānqì tài lěng le.

(It's too cold yesterday.)

02

A: Xiànzài nǐ zěnmeyàng?

(How do you feel now?)

B: Wǒ
tóu téng *(headache)*
sǎngzi téng *(sore throat)*
fāshāo *(fever)*
.

A: Jīntiān nǐ qù gōngzuò ma?

(Are you going to work today?)

Nǐ xiūxi xiūxi ba.

(You'd better have a rest.)

Notes

1. "le" is used at the end of a sentence, indicating a change has been completed.

2. Sometimes we repeat the verb to indicate an informal, casual tone of voice such as:

① qíqi zìxíngchē *(ride bike)*

② hēhe píjiǔ *(drink beer)*

3. "ba" can be used at the end of a sentence to indicate a suggestion. For example:

① Qù chāoshì ba. *(Let's go to the supermarket.)*

② Nǐ chī píngguǒ ba. *(Please eat an apple.)*

Unit 7

What is your hobby?

What do you like to do in your spare time? We have so many choices nowadays and lead such colorful lives. In this unit, we are going to talk about weekday pastimes, sports, TV programs, and some other activities related to the Internet, reading, music, and travel!

中文入门

Chinese For Beginners

What is your hobby?

PAGE

7-1

What day is it today?

Weekdays

xīngqīyī	星期一 MONDAY
xīngqī'èr	星期二 TUESDAY
xīngqīsān	星期三 WEDNESDAY
xīngqīsì	星期四 THURSDAY
xīngqīwǔ	星期五 FRIDAY
xīngqīliù	星期六 SATURDAY
xīngqītiān	星期天 SUNDAY

Dialogues

01

A: Jīntiān (shì) xīngqījǐ?

(What day is it today?)

B: Jīntiān (shì) xīngqīyī.

(Today is Monday.)

02

A: Xīngqī'èr nǐ yǒu shíjiān ma?

(Do you have time on Tuesday?)

B: Yǒu, shénme shì?

(Yes, why?)

A: Wǒmen yìqǐ chī wǔfàn, hǎo ma?

(Let's have lunch together.)

B: Hǎo, jǐ diǎn?

(OK. When?)

A: Shí'èr diǎn.

(Twelve o'clock.)

03

A: Xīngqīwǔ nǐ yǒu shíjiān ma?

(Do you have time on Friday?)

B: Duìbuqǐ, wǒ méiyǒu shíjiān.

(Sorry. I have no time.)

A: Méi guānxi.

(Never mind.)

Notes

1. "men" is a noun suffix denoting plurality, only used after personal pronouns or nouns. For example:

wǒ *(I,me)*	wǒmen *(we,us)*
nǐ *(you)*	nǐmen *(you)*
tā *(he,him,she,her)*	tāmen *(they, them)*
lǎoshī *(teacher)*	lǎoshīmen *(teachers)*
xuésheng *(student)*	xuéshengmen *(students)*

2. A noun can act as the predicate to indicate weather, time, age, price, etc. For example:

① Míngtiān qíngtiān. *(Tomorrow is a sunny day.)*

② Jīntiān xīngqīliù. *(Today is Saturday.)*

③ Zhè ge èrshí kuài. *(This is 20 dollars.)*

④ Tā èrshíyī suì. *(He is 21 years old.)*

Some verbs can be used in the sentences, such as "shì" for the above ones:

① Míngtiān shì qíngtiān. *(Tomorrow is a sunny day.)*

② Jīntiān shì xīngqīliù. *(Today is Saturday.)*

③ Zhè ge shì èrshí kuài. *(This is 20 dollars.)*

④ Tā shì èrshíyī suì. *(He is 21 years old.)*

So if you want to give the negative sentence, the proper verb must be used. For the above sentences for example:

① Míngtiān búshì qíngtiān. *(Tomorrow is not a sunny day.)*

② Jīntiān búshì xīngqīliù. *(Today is not Saturday.)*

③ Zhè ge búshì èrshí kuài. *(This is not 20 dollars.)*

④ Tā búshì èrshíyī suì. *(He is not 21 years old.)*

I like swimming.

Dialogues

01

A: Nǐ xǐhuan shénme yùndòng?

(What sports do you like?)

B: Wǒ xǐhuan ... .

(I like...)

dǎ lánqiú	*(playing basketball)*
pǎobù	*(running)*
yóuyǒng	*(swimming)*
tī zúqiú	*(playing soccer)*
qí zìxíngchē	*(bicycling)*

02

A: Nǐ měi tiān dǎ lánqiú ma?

(Do you play basketball every day?)

B: Wǒ měi tiān xiàwǔ dǎ lánqiú.

(I play basketball in the afternoon every day.)

7-3 I watch TV news every day.

Dialogues

01

A: Nǐ kàn diànshì ma?

(Do you watch TV?)

B: Wǒ měi tiān zǎoshang kàn xīnwén.

(I watch TV news in the morning every day.)

02

A: Nǐ xǐhuan kàn shénme jiémù?

(What program do you like to watch?)

B: Wǒ xǐhuan kàn yīnyuè jiémù.

(I like to watch music program.)

Wǒ měi tiān wǎnshang

(Every night I...)

kàn *(watch)*	yīnyuè jiémù	*(music program)*	.
	tǐyù bǐsài	*(sports match)*	
	dònghuàpiàn	*(cartoon)*	
	jìlùpiàn	*(documentary)*	
	diànshìjù	*(TV series)*	
	diànyǐng	*(movie)*	

7-4

We can do a lot of things through Internet.

Expressions

1. Zhèli néng shàng wǎng ma?
Wǒ yào kàn yóujiàn.

(Can I surf the Internet here?
I need to check my e-mail.)

2. Wǒ chángcháng

(I often...)

shàng wǎng *(go online)*

- kàn xīnwén *(read the news)*
- liáotiān *(chat)*
- gòuwù *(shop)*
- wánr yóuxì *(play games)*

.

Dialogue

01

A: Nǐ yǒu shénme àihào?
(What's your hobby?)

B: Wǒ xǐhuan....
(I like...)

kàn shū *(reading)*
tīng yīnyuè *(listening to music)* .
lǚxíng *(traveling)*

中文入门 ➤➤➤

Vocabulary List

Pinyin	character	English	Spanish	unit-lecture
àihào	爱好	hobby	afición	7-4
bàba	爸爸	father	papá	1-4
ba	吧	(particle)	(partícula)	6-4
bái	白	white	blanco	4-1
bāozi	包子	steamed stuffed bun	empanada chinas	3-1
bù	不	no	no	1-3
bú kèqi	不客气	You are welcome	De nada.	5-4
chá	茶	tea	té	3-4
chángcháng	常常	often	a menudo	7-4
chāoshì	超市	supermarket	supermercado	5-2
chǎofàn	炒饭	fried rice	arroz frito	3-1
chǎomiàn	炒面	stir-fried noodles	tallarines fritos	3-1
chéngzi	橙子	orange	naranja	3-2
chī	吃	eat	comer	2-4
chūntiān	春天	spring	primavera	6-3
dǎ lánqiú	打篮球	play basketball	jugar al baloncesto	7-2
dà	大	big	grande	4-2
de	的	(particle)	(partícula)	4-1
dìtiě	地铁	underground	metro	5-1
dìtiězhàn	地铁站	underground station	La estación de metro	5-2
dìdi	弟弟	younger brother	hermano menor	1-4
diǎn	点	o'clock	hora	2-2
diànshì	电视	television	tele	7-3

Pinyin	character	English	Spanish	unit-lecture
diànshìjù	电视剧	TV series	serie de televisión	7-3
diànyǐng	电影	film	película	7-3
dōngtiān	冬天	winter	invierno	6-3
dònghuàpiàn	动画片	cartoon	dibujos animados	7-3
dù	度	degree	grado	6-1
duì	对	right	sí	1-3
duìbuqǐ	对不起	sorry	perdón	5-2
duōshao	多少	how many; how much	cuánto,ta	4-3
fāshāo	发烧	have a fever	tener fiebre	6-4
fùjìn	附近	nearby	cerca	5-2
gǎnmào	感冒	catch a cold	resfriado,da	6-4
gēge	哥哥	elder brother	hermano mayor	1-4
gè	个	(measure word)	(medidor)	4-2
gōngzuò	工作	work	trabajar, trabajo	2-4
gōnggòng qìchē	公共汽车	bus	autobús	5-1
gòuwù	购物	shop	ir de compras	7-4
guǎi	拐	turn	girar	5-4
guì	贵	expensive	caro,ra	4-4
guó	国	country	país	1-2
Hànyǔ	汉语	Chinese language	chino	1-3
hǎo	好	good	bueno,na	1-1
hē	喝	drink	beber	3-4

Pinyin	character	English	Spanish	unit-lecture
hēi	黑	black	negro,gra	4-1
hěn	很	very	muy	6-1
hóng	红	red	rojo,ja	4-1
hòubian	后边	backward	atrás	5-3
huáng	黄	yellow	amarillo,lla	4-1
huíjiā	回家	go home	volver a casa	2-4
jīròu	鸡肉	chicken	pollo	3-3
jǐ	几	how many	cuántos,as	2-2
jìlùpiàn	纪录片	documentary	documental	7-3
jìjié	季节	season	estación	6-3
jiàn	件	(measure word for clothing)	(medidor para ropa)	4-2
jiǎozi	饺子	dumpling	empanadillas chinas	3-1
jiào	叫	call	llamar	1-1
jiémù	节目	program	programa	7-3
jiějie	姐姐	elder sister	hermana mayor	1-4
jīntiān	今天	today	hoy	6-1
kāfēi	咖啡	coffee	café	3-4
kāi chē	开车	drive a car	conducir un coche	5-1
kàn	看	look; watch	mirar	7-3
kànshū	看书	read a book	leer un libro	7-4
kělè	可乐	coke	Coca-Cola	3-4
kuài	块	(measure word for money)	(medidor para dinero)	4-3

Pinyin	character	English	Spanish	unit-lecture
lán	蓝	blue	azul	4-1
lǎoshī	老师	teacher	profesor	1-3
le	了	(particle)	(partícula)	6-4
lěng	冷	cold	frío	6-1
liáotiān	聊天	chat	charlar	7-4
lǚxíng	旅行	travel	viajar	7-4
lǜ	绿	green	verde	4-1
māma	妈妈	mother	mamá	1-4
ma	吗	(particle)	(partícula)	1-3
méi guānxi	没关系	Never mind	No importa.	5-2
méiyǒu	没有	have no	no tener	7-1
měi tiān	每天	every day	todos los días	5-1
mèimei	妹妹	younger sister	hermana menor	1-4
miàntiáo	面条	noodles	tallarines	3-1
míngzi	名字	name	nombre	1-1
míngtiān	明天	tomorrow	mañana	6-1
nǎ	哪	which	cuál	1-2
nǎr	哪儿	where	dónde	5-3
nà	那	that	ese,esa,ése, ésa,eso	4-2
nàr	那儿	there	ahí, allí	5-2
néng	能	can	poder	7-4
nǐ	你	you	tú	1-1
niúròu	牛肉	beef	ternera	3-3

Pinyin	character	English	Spanish	unit-lecture
pǎobù	跑步	run	correr	7-2
píjiǔ	啤酒	beer	cerveza	3-4
piányi	便宜	cheap	barato	4-4
píngguǒ	苹果	apple	manzana	3-2
qí zìxíngchē	骑自行车	ride a bike	montar en bici	5-1
qǐchuáng	起床	get up	levantarse	2-4
qiánbian	前边	front	delante	5-3
qián	钱	money	dinero	4-3
qǐngwèn	请问	Excuse me	perdón	2-2
qiūtiān	秋天	autumn	otoño	6-3
qù	去	go	ir	5-1
rè	热	warm; hot	calor	6-1
rén	人	person	gente	1-2
sǎngzi	嗓子	throat	garganta	6-4
shāngdiàn	商店	shop	tienda	5-2
shàngbian	上边	up; above	sobre	5-3
shàngwǎng	上网	surf Internet	navegar por internet	7-4
shàngwǔ	上午	morning	mañana	2-3
shénme	什么	what	qué	1-1
shíjiān	时间	time	tiempo	7-1
shì	事	matter	asunto	7-1
shì	是	be	ser, estar	1-2
shūcài	蔬菜	vegetable	verdura	3-3

Pinyin	character	English	Spanish	unit-lecture
shéi	谁	who	quién	1-4
shuǐ	水	water	agua	3-4
shuǐguǒ	水果	fruit	fruta	3-2
shuìjiào	睡觉	sleep	dormir	2-4
tā /tā	他/她	he/she	él/ella	1-4
tài……le	太……了	too; extremely	demasiado	4-2
tī zúqiú	踢足球	play football	jugar al fútbol	7-2
tǐyù bǐsài	体育比赛	sports match	partido	7-3
tiānqì	天气	weather	tiempo	6-1
tīng	听	listen	escuchar	7-4
tóuténg	头疼	headache	el dolor de cabeza	6-4
wánr yóuxì	玩儿游戏	play a game	jugar a juego	7-4
wǎnfàn	晚饭	supper; dinner	cena	2-4
wǎnshang	晚上	evening; night	noche	2-3
wǎng	往	toward	hacia	5-4
wèi shénme	为什么	why	por qué	6-3
wǒ	我	I	yo	1-1
wǒmen	我们	we	nosotros	7-1
wǔfàn	午饭	lunch	almuerzo	7-1
xǐshǒujiān	洗手间	restroom	cuarto de baño	5-4
xǐhuan	喜欢	like	gustar	3-2
xiàbian	下边	down; below	abajo	5-3
xiàwǔ	下午	afternoon	tarde	2-3

Pinyin	character	English	Spanish	unit-lecture
xiàxuě	下雪	snow	nevar	6-1
xiàyǔ	下雨	rain	llover	6-1
xiàtiān	夏天	summer	verano	6-3
xiànzài	现在	now	ahora	2-2
xiāngjiāo	香蕉	banana	plátano	3-2
xiǎo	小	small	pequeño	4-2
xièxie	谢谢	thanks	gracias	1-1
xīnwén	新闻	news	noticias	7-3
xīngqī	星期	week	semana	7-1
xiūxi	休息	have a rest	descansar	6-4
xuésheng	学生	student	estudiante	1-3
xuéxí	学习	learn; study	estudiar	1-3
xuéxiào	学校	school	escuela	5-1
yánsè	颜色	color	color	4-1
yào	要	want	querer	3-3
yìdiǎnr	一点儿	a little; some	un poco	4-4
yìqǐ	一起	together	juntos	7-1
yīnwèi	因为	because	porque	6-3
yīnyuè	音乐	music	música	7-3
yínháng	银行	bank	banco	5-2
yóujiàn	邮件	mail	correo	7-4
yóuyǒng	游泳	swim	nadar	7-2
yǒu	有	have	tener	5-2

Pinyin	character	English	Spanish	unit-lecture
yòubian	右边	right side	derecho	5-4
yú	鱼	fish	pescado	3-3
yuè	月	month	mes	6-2
yùndòng	运动	sports	deporte	7-2
zàijiàn	再见	good-bye	adiós	1-1
zài	在	be in; be at	estar en	5-2
zǎofàn	早饭	breakfast	desayuno	2-4
zǎoshang	早上	early morning	mañana	2-3
zěnme	怎么	how	cómo	5-1
zěnmeyàng	怎么样	how about	qué tal	4-2
zhè	这	this	este,esta, éste,ésta,esto	1-4
zhèli	这里	here	aquí	7-4
zhīdào	知道	know	saber,conocer	5-2
zhōngwǔ	中午	noon	mediodía	2-3
zhūròu	猪肉	pork	cerdo	3-3
zǒu	走	go	ir	5-4
zǒulù	走路	walk	caminar	5-1
zuótiān	昨天	yesterday	ayer	6-4
zuǒbian	左边	left side	izquierdo,da	5-4
zuò	坐	sit	sentarse	5-1

Numbers

Pinyin	character	English	Spanish	unit-lecture
yī	一	one	uno	2-1
èr	二	two	dos	2-1
sān	三	three	tres	2-1
sì	四	four	cuatro	2-1
wǔ	五	five	cinco	2-1
liù	六	six	seis	2-1
qī	七	seven	siete	2-1
bā	八	eight	ocho	2-1
jiǔ	九	nine	nueve	2-1
shí	十	ten	diez	2-1

INSTRUCTIONS

STEP1. READ THE BOOK

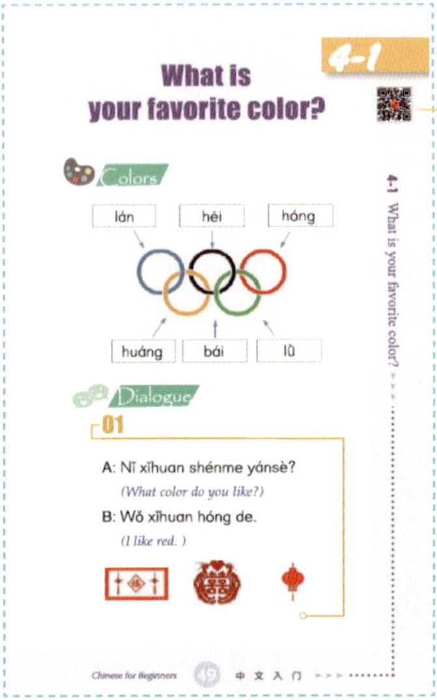
4-1

What is your favorite color?

Colors

lán hēi hóng

huáng bái lǜ

Dialogue

01

A: Nǐ xǐhuan shénme yánsè?

(What color do you like?)

B: Wǒ xǐhuan hóng de.

(I like red.)

4-1 What is your favorite color?

Chinese for Beginners 49 中文入门

STEP2. SCAN THE QR CODE HE

STEP4. REVIEW THE BOOK

STEP3. WATCH THE VIDEO HERE